QUAS PRIMAS

On the

Christ the King
by
Pope Pius XI
1925

St Athanasius Press

ISBN-13: 978-1533145994

ISBN-10: 1533145997

St Athanasius Press
2016

Specializing in Reprinting Catholic Classics!

QUAS PRIMAS

ENCYCLICAL OF POPE PIUS XI ON THE FEAST OF CHRIST THE KING

TO OUR VENERABLE BRETHREN THE PATRIARCHS, PRIMATES, ARCHBISHOPS, BISHOPS, AND OTHER ORDINARIES IN PEACE AND COMMUNION WITH THE APOSTOLIC SEE.

Venerable Brethren, Greeting and the Apostolic Benediction.

In the first Encyclical Letter which We addressed at the beginning of Our Pontificate to the Bishops of the universal Church, We referred to the chief causes of the difficulties under which mankind was laboring. And We remember saying that these manifold evils in the world were due to the fact that the majority of men had thrust Jesus Christ and his holy law out of their lives; that these had no place either in private affairs or in politics: and we said further, that as long as individuals and states refused to submit to the rule of our Savior, there would be no really hopeful prospect of a lasting peace among nations. Men must look for the peace of Christ in the Kingdom of Christ; and that We promised to do as far as lay in Our power. In the Kingdom of Christ, that is, it seemed to Us that peace could not be more effectually restored nor fixed upon a firmer basis than through the restoration of the Empire of Our Lord. We were led in the meantime to indulge the hope of a brighter future at the sight of a more widespread and keener interest evinced in Christ and his Church, the one Source of Salvation, a sign that men who had formerly spurned the rule of our Redeemer and had exiled themselves from his kingdom were preparing, and even hastening, to return to the duty of obedience.

2. The many notable and memorable events which have occurred during this Holy Year have given great honor and glory to Our Lord and King, the Founder of the Church.

3. At the Missionary Exhibition men have been deeply impressed in seeing the increasing zeal of the Church for the spread of the kingdom of her Spouse to the most far distant regions of the earth. They have seen how many countries have been won to the Catholic name through the unremitting labor and self-sacrifice of missionaries, and the vastness of the regions which have yet to be subjected to the sweet and saving yoke of our King. All those who in the course of the Holy Year have thronged to this

city under the leadership of their Bishops or priests had but one aim - namely, to expiate their sins - and at the tombs of the Apostles and in Our Presence to promise loyalty to the rule of Christ.

4. A still further light of glory was shed upon his kingdom, when after due proof of their heroic virtue, We raised to the honors of the altar six confessors and virgins. It was a great joy, a great consolation, that filled Our heart when in the majestic basilica of St. Peter Our decree was acclaimed by an immense multitude with the hymn of thanksgiving, Tu Rex gloriae Christe. We saw men and nations cut off from God, stirring up strife and discord and hurrying along the road to ruin and death, while the Church of God carries on her work of providing food for the spiritual life of men, nurturing and fostering generation after generation of men and women dedicated to Christ,

faithful and subject to him in his earthly kingdom, called by him to eternal bliss in the kingdom of heaven.

5. Moreover, since this jubilee Year marks the sixteenth centenary of the Council of Nicaea, We commanded that event to be celebrated, and We have done so in the Vatican basilica. There is a special reason for this in that the Nicene Synod defined and proposed for Catholic belief the dogma of the Consubstantiality of the Only begotten with the Father, and added to the Creed the words "of whose kingdom there shall be no end," thereby affirming the kingly dignity of Christ.

6. Since this Holy Year therefore has provided more than one opportunity to enhance the glory of the kingdom of Christ, we deem it in keeping with our Apostolic office to accede to the desire

of many of the Cardinals, Bishops, and faithful, made known to Us both individually and collectively, by closing this Holy Year with the insertion into the Sacred Liturgy of a special feast of the Kingship of Our Lord Jesus Christ. This matter is so dear to Our heart, Venerable Brethren, that I would wish to address to you a few words concerning it. It will be for you later to explain in a manner suited to the understanding of the faithful what We are about to say concerning the Kingship of Christ, so that the annual feast which We shall decree may be attended with much fruit and produce beneficial results in the future.

7. It has long been a common custom to give to Christ the metaphorical title of "King," because of the high degree of perfection whereby he excels all creatures. So he is said to reign "in the hearts of men," both by reason of the keen-

ness of his intellect and the extent of his knowledge, and also because he is very truth, and it is from him that truth must be obediently received by all mankind. He reigns, too, in the wills of men, for in him the human will was perfectly and entirely obedient to the Holy Will of God, and further by his grace and inspiration he so subjects our free-will as to incite us to the most noble endeavors. He is King of hearts, too, by reason of his "charity which exceedeth all knowledge." And his mercy and kindness which draw all men to him, for never has it been known, nor will it ever be, that man be loved so much and so universally as Jesus Christ. But if we ponder this matter more deeply, we cannot but see that the title and the power of King belongs to Christ as man in the strict and proper sense too. For it is only as man that he may be said to have received from the Father "power and glory and a kingdom," since the Word of God, as consubstantial with the Father, has all things in common with him, and therefore has necessarily supreme and absolute dominion over all things created.

8. Do we not read throughout the Scriptures that Christ is the King? He it is that shall come out of Jacob to rule, who has been set by the Father as king over Sion, his holy mount, and shall have the Gentiles for his inheritance, and the utmost parts of the earth for his possession. In the nuptial hymn, where the future King of Israel is hailed as a most rich and powerful monarch, we read: "Thy throne, O God, is for ever and ever; the scepter of thy kingdom is a scepter of righteousness." There are many similar passages, but there is one in which Christ is even more clearly indicated. Here it is foretold that his kingdom will have no limits, and will be enriched

with justice and peace: "in his days shall justice spring up, and abundance of peace...And he shall rule from sea to sea, and from the river unto the ends of the earth."

9. The testimony of the Prophets is even more abundant. That of Isaias is well known: "For a child is born to us and a son is given to us, and the government is upon his shoulder, and his name shall be called Wonderful, Counselor, God the mighty, the Father of the world to come, the Prince of Peace. His empire shall be multiplied, and there shall be no end of peace. He shall sit upon the throne of David and upon his kingdom; to establish it and strengthen it with judgment and with justice, from henceforth and forever." With Isaias the other Prophets are in agreement. So Jeremias foretells the "just seed" that shall rest from the house of David - the Son of David that

shall reign as king, "and shall be wise, and shall execute judgment and justice in the earth." So, too, Daniel, who announces the kingdom that the God of heaven shall found, "that shall never be destroyed, and shall stand for ever." And again he says: "I beheld, therefore, in the vision of the night, and, lo! one like the son of man came with the clouds of heaven. And he came even to the Ancient of days: and they presented him before him. And he gave him power and glory and a kingdom: and all peoples, tribes, and tongues shall serve him. His power is an everlasting power that shall not be taken away, and his kingdom shall not be destroyed." The prophecy of Zachary concerning the merciful King "riding upon an ass and upon a colt the foal of an ass" entering Jerusalem as "the just and savior," amid the acclamations of the multitude, was recognized as fulfilled by the holy evangelists themselves.

10. This same doctrine of the Kingship of Christ which we have found in the Old Testament is even more clearly taught and confirmed in the New. The Archangel, announcing to the Virgin that she should bear a Son, says that "the Lord God shall give unto him the throne of David his father, and he shall reign in the house of Jacob forever; and of his kingdom there shall be no end."

11. Moreover, Christ himself speaks of his own kingly authority: in his last discourse, speaking of the rewards and punishments that will be the eternal lot of the just and the damned; in his reply to the Roman magistrate, who asked him publicly whether he were a king or not; after his resurrection, when giving to his Apostles the mission of teaching and baptizing all nations, he took the opportunity to call himself king, confirming the title publicly, and solemnly

proclaimed that all power was given him in heaven and on earth. These words can only be taken to indicate the greatness of his power, the infinite extent of his kingdom. What wonder, then, that he whom St. John calls the "prince of the kings of the earth" appears in the Apostle's vision of the future as he who "hath on his garment and on his thigh written 'King of kings and Lord of lords!'." It is Christ whom the Father "hath appointed heir of all things"; "for he must reign until at the end of the world he hath put all his enemies under the feet of God and the Father."

12. It was surely right, then, in view of the common teaching of the sacred books, that the Catholic Church, which is the kingdom of Christ on earth, destined to be spread among all men and all nations, should with every token of veneration salute her Author and Founder in

her annual liturgy as King and Lord, and as King of Kings. And, in fact, she used these titles, giving expression with wonderful variety of language to one and the same concept, both in ancient psalmody and in the Sacramentaries. She uses them daily now in the prayers publicly offered to God, and in offering the Immaculate Victim. The perfect harmony of the Eastern liturgies with our own in this continual praise of Christ the King shows once more the truth of the axiom: Legem credendi lex statuit supplicandi. The rule of faith is indicated by the law of our worship.

13. The foundation of this power and dignity of Our Lord is rightly indicated by Cyril of Alexandria. "Christ," he says, "has dominion over all creatures, a dominion not seized by violence nor usurped, but his by essence and by nature." His kingship is founded upon the

ineffable hypostatic union. From this it follows not only that Christ is to be adored by angels and men, but that to him as man angels and men are subject, and must recognize his empire; by reason of the hypostatic union Christ has power over all creatures. But a thought that must give us even greater joy and consolation is this that Christ is our King by acquired, as well as by natural right, for he is our Redeemer. Would that they who forget what they have cost their Savior might recall the words: "You were not redeemed with corruptible things, but with the precious blood of Christ, as of a lamb unspotted and undefiled." We are no longer our own property, for Christ has purchased us "with a great price"; our very bodies are the "members of Christ."

14. Let Us explain briefly the nature and meaning of this lordship of Christ.

It consists, We need scarcely say, in a threefold power which is essential to lordship. This is sufficiently clear from the scriptural testimony already adduced concerning the universal dominion of our Redeemer, and moreover it is a dogma of faith that Jesus Christ was given to man, not only as our Redeemer, but also as a law-giver, to whom obedience is due. Not only do the gospels tell us that he made laws, but they present him to us in the act of making them. Those who keep them show their love for their Divine Master, and he promises that they shall remain in his love. He claimed judicial power as received from his Father, when the Jews accused him of breaking the Sabbath by the miraculous cure of a sick man. "For neither doth the Father judge any man; but hath given all judgment to the Son." In this power is included the right of rewarding and punishing all men living, for this right is inseparable from that of judging. Executive power, too, belongs to Christ, for all must obey his commands; none may escape them, nor the sanctions he has imposed.

15. This kingdom is spiritual and is concerned with spiritual things. That this is so the above quotations from Scripture amply prove, and Christ by his own action confirms it. On many occasions, when the Jews and even the Apostles wrongly supposed that the Messiah would restore the liberties and the kingdom of Israel, he repelled and denied such a suggestion. When the populace thronged around him in admiration and would have acclaimed him King, he shrank from the honor and sought safety in flight. Before the Roman magistrate he declared that his kingdom was not of this world. The gospels present this kingdom as one which men prepare to enter

by penance, and cannot actually enter except by faith and by baptism, which, though an external rite, signifies and produces an interior regeneration. This kingdom is opposed to none other than to that of Satan and to the power of darkness. It demands of its subjects a spirit of detachment from riches and earthly things, and a spirit of gentleness. They must hunger and thirst after justice, and more than this, they must deny themselves and carry the cross.

16. Christ as our Redeemer purchased the Church at the price of his own blood; as priest he offered himself, and continues to offer himself as a victim for our sins. Is it not evident, then, that his kingly dignity partakes in a manner of both these offices?

17. It would be a grave error, on the other hand, to say that Christ has no au-

thority whatever in civil affairs, since, by virtue of the absolute empire over all creatures committed to him by the Father, all things are in his power. Nevertheless, during his life on earth he refrained from the exercise of such authority, and although he himself disdained to possess or to care for earthly goods, he did not, nor does he today, interfere with those who possess them. Non eripit mortalia qui regna dat caelestia.

18. Thus the empire of our Redeemer embraces all men. To use the words of Our immortal predecessor, Pope Leo XIII: "His empire includes not only Catholic nations, not only baptized persons who, though of right belonging to the Church, have been led astray by error, or have been cut off from her by schism, but also all those who are outside the Christian faith; so that truly the whole of mankind is subject to the pow-

er of Jesus Christ." Nor is there any difference in this matter between the individual and the family or the State; for all men, whether collectively or individually, are under the dominion of Christ. In him is the salvation of the individual, in him is the salvation of society. "Neither is there salvation in any other, for there is no other name under heaven given to men whereby we must be saved." He is the author of happiness and true prosperity for every man and for every nation. "For a nation is happy when its citizens are happy. What else is a nation but a number of men living in concord?" If, therefore, the rulers of nations wish to preserve their authority, to promote and increase the prosperity of their countries, they will not neglect the public duty of reverence and obedience to the rule of Christ. What We said at the beginning of Our Pontificate concerning the decline of public authority, and the lack of respect for the same, is equally true at the present day. "With God and Jesus Christ," we said, "excluded from political life, with authority derived not from God but from man, the very basis of that authority has been taken away, because the chief reason of the distinction between ruler and subject has been eliminated. The result is that human society is tottering to its fall, because it has no longer a secure and solid foundation."

19. When once men recognize, both in private and in public life, that Christ is King, society will at last receive the great blessings of real liberty, well-ordered discipline, peace and harmony. Our Lord's regal office invests the human authority of princes and rulers with a religious significance; it ennobles the citizen's duty of obedience. It is for this reason that St. Paul, while bidding wives revere Christ in their husbands,

and slaves respect Christ in their masters, warns them to give obedience to them not as men, but as the vicegerents of Christ; for it is not meet that men redeemed by Christ should serve their fellow-men. "You are bought with a price; be not made the bond-slaves of men." If princes and magistrates duly elected are filled with the persuasion that they rule, not by their own right, but by the mandate and in the place of the Divine King, they will exercise their authority piously and wisely, and they will make laws and administer them, having in view the common good and also the human dignity of their subjects. The result will be a stable peace and tranquility, for there will be no longer any cause of discontent. Men will see in their king or in their rulers men like themselves, perhaps unworthy or open to criticism, but they will not on that account refuse obedience if they see reflected in them the authority of Christ God and Man. Peace and harmony, too, will result; for with the spread and the universal extent of the kingdom of Christ men will become more and more conscious of the link that binds them together, and thus many conflicts will be either prevented entirely or at least their bitterness will be diminished.

20. If the kingdom of Christ, then, receives, as it should, all nations under its way, there seems no reason why we should despair of seeing that peace which the King of Peace came to bring on earth - he who came to reconcile all things, who came not to be ministered unto but to minister, who, though Lord of all, gave himself to us as a model of humility, and with his principal law united the precept of charity; who said also: "My yoke is sweet and my burden light." Oh, what happiness would be Ours if all

men, individuals, families, and nations, would but let themselves be governed by Christ! "Then at length," to use the words addressed by our predecessor, Pope Leo XIII, twenty-five years ago to the bishops of the Universal Church, "then at length will many evils be cured; then will the law regain its former authority; peace with all its blessings be restored. Men will sheathe their swords and lay down their arms when all freely acknowledge and obey the authority of Christ, and every tongue confesses that the Lord Jesus Christ is in the glory of God the Father."

21. That these blessings may be abundant and lasting in Christian society, it is necessary that the kingship of our Savior should be as widely as possible recognized and understood, and to the end nothing would serve better than the institution of a special feast in honor

of the Kingship of Christ. For people are instructed in the truths of faith, and brought to appreciate the inner joys of religion far more effectually by the annual celebration of our sacred mysteries than by any official pronouncement of the teaching of the Church. Such pronouncements usually reach only a few and the more learned among the faithful; feasts reach them all; the former speak but once, the latter speak every year - in fact, forever. The church's teaching affects the mind primarily; her feasts affect both mind and heart, and have a salutary effect upon the whole of man's nature. Man is composed of body and soul, and he needs these external festivities so that the sacred rites, in all their beauty and variety, may stimulate him to drink more deeply of the fountain of God's teaching, that he may make it a part of himself, and use it with profit for his spiritual life.

22. History, in fact, tells us that in the course of ages these festivals have been instituted one after another according as the needs or the advantage of the people of Christ seemed to demand: as when they needed strength to face a common danger, when they were attacked by insidious heresies, when they needed to be urged to the pious consideration of some mystery of faith or of some divine blessing. Thus in the earliest days of the Christian era, when the people of Christ were suffering cruel persecution, the cult of the martyrs was begun in order, says St. Augustine, "that the feasts of the martyrs might incite men to martyrdom." The liturgical honors paid to confessors, virgins and widows produced wonderful results in an increased zest for virtue, necessary even in times of peace. But more fruitful still were the feasts instituted in honor of the Blessed Virgin. As a result of these men grew

not only in their devotion to the Mother of God as an ever-present advocate, but also in their love of her as a mother bequeathed to them by their Redeemer. Not least among the blessings which have resulted from the public and legitimate honor paid to the Blessed Virgin and the saints is the perfect and perpetual immunity of the Church from error and heresy. We may well admire in this the admirable wisdom of the Providence of God, who, ever bringing good out of evil, has from time to time suffered the faith and piety of men to grow weak, and allowed Catholic truth to be attacked by false doctrines, but always with the result that truth has afterwards shone out with greater splendor, and that men's faith, aroused from its lethargy, has shown itself more vigorous than before.

23. The festivals that have been introduced into the liturgy in more recent

years have had a similar origin, and have been attended with similar results. When reverence and devotion to the Blessed Sacrament had grown cold, the feast of Corpus Christi was instituted, so that by means of solemn processions and prayer of eight days' duration, men might be brought once more to render public homage to Christ. So, too, the feast of the Sacred Heart of Jesus was instituted at a time when men were oppressed by the sad and gloomy severity of Jansenism, which had made their hearts grow cold, and shut them out from the love of God and the hope of salvation.

24. If We ordain that the whole Catholic world shall revere Christ as King, We shall minister to the need of the present day, and at the same time provide an excellent remedy for the plague which now infects society. We refer to the plague of anti-clericalism, its errors and impi-

ous activities. This evil spirit, as you are well aware, Venerable Brethren, has not come into being in one day; it has long lurked beneath the surface. The empire of Christ over all nations was rejected. The right which the Church has from Christ himself, to teach mankind, to make laws, to govern peoples in all that pertains to their eternal salvation that right was denied. Then gradually the religion of Christ came to be likened to false religions and to be placed ignominiously on the same level with them. It was then put under the power of the state and tolerated more or less at the whim of princes and rulers. Some men went even further, and wished to set up in the place of God's religion a natural religion consisting in some instinctive affection of the heart. There were even some nations who thought they could dispense with God, and that their religion should consist in impiety and the neglect of God.

The rebellion of individuals and states against the authority of Christ has produced deplorable consequences. We lamented these in the Encyclical Ubi arcano; we lament them today: the seeds of discord sown far and wide; those bitter enmities and rivalries between nations, which still hinder so much the cause of peace; that insatiable greed which is so often hidden under a pretense of public spirit and patriotism, and gives rise to so many private quarrels; a blind and immoderate selfishness, making men seek nothing but their own comfort and advantage, and measure everything by these; no peace in the home, because men have forgotten or neglect their duty; the unity and stability of the family undermined; society in a word, shaken to its foundations and on the way to ruin. We firmly hope, however, that the feast of the Kingship of Christ, which in future will be yearly observed, may hasten the return of society to our loving Savior. It would be the duty of Catholics to do all they can to bring about this happy result. Many of these, however, have neither the station in society nor the authority which should belong to those who bear the torch of truth. This state of things may perhaps be attributed to a certain slowness and timidity in good people, who are reluctant to engage in conflict or oppose but a weak resistance; thus the enemies of the Church become bolder in their attacks. But if the faithful were generally to understand that it behooves them ever to fight courageously under the banner of Christ their King, then, fired with apostolic zeal, they would strive to win over to their Lord those hearts that are bitter and estranged from him, and would valiantly defend his rights.

25. Moreover, the annual and univer-

sal celebration of the feast of the Kingship of Christ will draw attention to the evil which anticlericalism has brought upon society in drawing men away from Christ, and will also do much to remedy them. While nations insult the beloved name of our Redeemer by suppressing all mention of it in their conferences and parliaments, we must all the more loudly proclaim his kingly dignity and power, all the more universally affirm his rights.

26. The way has been happily and providentially prepared for the celebration of this feast ever since the end of the last century. It is well known that this cult has been the subject of learned disquisitions in many books published in every part of the world, written in many different languages. The kingship and empire of Christ have been recognized in the pious custom, practiced by many families, of dedicating themselves to the

Sacred Heart of Jesus; not only families have performed this act of dedication, but nations, too, and kingdoms. In fact, the whole of the human race was at the instance of Pope Leo XIII, in the Holy Year 1900, consecrated to the Divine Heart. It should be remarked also that much has been done for the recognition of Christ's authority over society by the frequent Eucharistic Congresses which are held in our age. These give an opportunity to the people of each diocese, district or nation, and to the whole world of coming together to venerate and adore Christ the King hidden under the Sacramental species. Thus by sermons preached at meetings and in churches, by public adoration of the Blessed Sacrament exposed and by solemn processions, men unite in paying homage to Christ, whom God has given them for their King. It is by a divine inspiration that the people of Christ bring forth Jesus from his silent hiding-place in the church, and carry him in triumph through the streets of the city, so that he whom men refused to receive when he came unto his own, may now receive in full his kingly rights.

27. For the fulfillment of the plan of which We have spoken, the Holy Year, which is now speeding to its close, offers the best possible opportunity. For during this year the God of mercy has raised the minds and hearts of the faithful to the consideration of heavenly blessings which are above all understanding, has either restored them once more to his grace, or inciting them anew to strive for higher gifts, has set their feet more firmly in the path of righteousness. Whether, therefore, We consider the many prayers that have been addressed to Us, or look to the events of the Jubilee Year, just past, We have every reason to think that

the desired moment has at length arrived for enjoining that Christ be venerated by a special feast as King of all mankind. In this year, as We said at the beginning of this Letter, the Divine King, truly wonderful in all his works, has been gloriously magnified, for another company of his soldiers has been added to the list of saints. In this year men have looked upon strange things and strange labors, from which they have understood and admired the victories won by missionaries in the work of spreading his kingdom. In this year, by solemnly celebrating the centenary of the Council of Nicaea, We have commemorated the definition of the divinity of the word Incarnate, the foundation of Christ's empire over all men.

28. Therefore by Our Apostolic Authority We institute the Feast of the Kingship of Our Lord Jesus Christ to be observed

yearly throughout the whole world on the last Sunday of the month of October - the Sunday, that is, which immediately precedes the Feast of All Saints. We further ordain that the dedication of mankind to the Sacred Heart of Jesus, which Our predecessor of saintly memory, Pope Pius X, commanded to be renewed yearly, be made annually on that day. This year, however, We desire that it be observed on the thirty-first day of the month on which day We Ourselves shall celebrate pontifically in honor of the kingship of Christ, and shall command that the same dedication be performed in Our presence. It seems to Us that We cannot in a more fitting manner close this Holy Year, nor better signify Our gratitude and that of the whole of the Catholic world to Christ the immortal King of ages, for the blessings showered upon Us, upon the Church, and upon the Catholic world during this holy period.

29. It is not necessary, Venerable Brethren, that We should explain to you at any length why We have decreed that this feast of the Kingship of Christ should be observed in addition to those other feasts in which his kingly dignity is already signified and celebrated. It will suffice to remark that although in all the feasts of our Lord the material object of worship is Christ, nevertheless their formal object is something quite distinct from his royal title and dignity. We have commanded its observance on a Sunday in order that not only the clergy may perform their duty by saying Mass and reciting the Office, but that the laity too, free from their daily tasks, may in a spirit of holy joy give ample testimony of their obedience and subjection to Christ. The last Sunday of October seemed the most convenient of all for this purpose, because it is at the end of the liturgical year, and thus the feast of the Kingship of Christ

sets the crowning glory upon the mysteries of the life of Christ already commemorated during the year, and, before celebrating the triumph of all the Saints, we proclaim and extol the glory of him who triumphs in all the Saints and in all the Elect. Make it your duty and your task, Venerable Brethren, to see that sermons are preached to the people in every parish to teach them the meaning and the importance of this feast, that they may so order their lives as to be worthy of faithful and obedient subjects of the Divine King.

30. We would now, Venerable Brethren, in closing this letter, briefly enumerate the blessings which We hope and pray may accrue to the Church, to society, and to each one of the faithful, as a result of the public veneration of the Kingship of Christ.

31. When we pay honor to the princely dignity of Christ, men will doubtless be reminded that the Church, founded by Christ as a perfect society, has a natural and inalienable right to perfect freedom and immunity from the power of the state; and that in fulfilling the task committed to her by God of teaching, ruling, and guiding to eternal bliss those who belong to the kingdom of Christ, she cannot be subject to any external power. The State is bound to extend similar freedom to the orders and communities of religious of either sex, who give most valuable help to the Bishops of the Church by laboring for the extension and the establishment of the kingdom of Christ. By their sacred vows they fight against the threefold concupiscence of the world; by making profession of a more perfect life they render the holiness which her divine Founder willed should be a mark and characteristic of

his Church more striking and more conspicuous in the eyes of all.

32. Nations will be reminded by the annual celebration of this feast that not only private individuals but also rulers and princes are bound to give public honor and obedience to Christ. It will call to their minds the thought of the last judgment, wherein Christ, who has been cast out of public life, despised, neglected and ignored, will most severely avenge these insults; for his kingly dignity demands that the State should take account of the commandments of God and of Christian principles, both in making laws and in administering justice, and also in providing for the young a sound moral education.

33. The faithful, moreover, by meditating upon these truths, will gain much strength and courage, enabling them to

form their lives after the true Christian ideal. If to Christ our Lord is given all power in heaven and on earth; if all men, purchased by his precious blood, are by a new right subjected to his dominion; if this power embraces all men, it must be clear that not one of our faculties is exempt from his empire. He must reign in our minds, which should assent with perfect submission and firm belief to revealed truths and to the doctrines of Christ. He must reign in our wills, which should obey the laws and precepts of God. He must reign in our hearts, which should spurn natural desires and love God above all things, and cleave to him alone. He must reign in our bodies and in our members, which should serve as instruments for the interior sanctification of our souls, or to use the words of the Apostle Paul, as instruments of justice unto God. If all these truths are presented to the faithful for their consideration, they will prove a powerful incentive to perfection. It is Our fervent desire, Venerable Brethren, that those who are without the fold may seek after and accept the sweet yoke of Christ, and that we, who by the mercy of God are of the household of the faith, may bear that yoke, not as a burden but with joy, with love, with devotion; that having lived our lives in accordance with the laws of God's kingdom, we may receive full measure of good fruit, and counted by Christ good and faithful servants, we may be rendered partakers of eternal bliss and glory with him in his heavenly kingdom.

34. Let this letter, Venerable Brethren, be a token to you of Our fatherly love as the Feast of the Nativity of Our Lord Jesus Christ draws near; and receive the Apostolic Benediction as a pledge of divine blessings, which with loving heart, We

impart to you, Venerable Brethren, to your clergy, and to your people.

Given at St. Peter's Rome, on the eleventh day of the month of December, in the Holy Year 1925, the fourth of Our Pontificate.

PIUS XI

Printed in Great Britain
by Amazon

11616666R00031